I0119573

F. (Francis) Sibson

Medical anatomy

Illustrations of the relative position and movements of the internal organs

F. (Francis) Sibson

Medical anatomy
Illustrations of the relative position and movements of the internal organs

ISBN/EAN: 9783742833877

Manufactured in Europe, USA, Canada, Australia, Japa

Cover: Foto ©Thomas Meinert / pixelio.de

Manufactured and distributed by brebook publishing software
(www.brebook.com)

F. (Francis) Sibson

Medical anatomy

OR,

ILLUSTRATIONS

OF THE

RELATIVE POSITION AND MOVEMENTS

OF THE

INTERNAL ORGANS.

BY

FRANCIS SIBSON, M.D. London and Dublin, F.R.S.;

Fellow of the Royal College of Physicians; Senior Physician to, and Lecturer on Clinical Medicine of, St. Mary's Hospital; Member of the Senate, and late Examiner in Medicine, of the University of London.

LONDON:

JOHN CHURCHILL & SONS, NEW BURLINGTON STREET.

MDCCCLXIX.

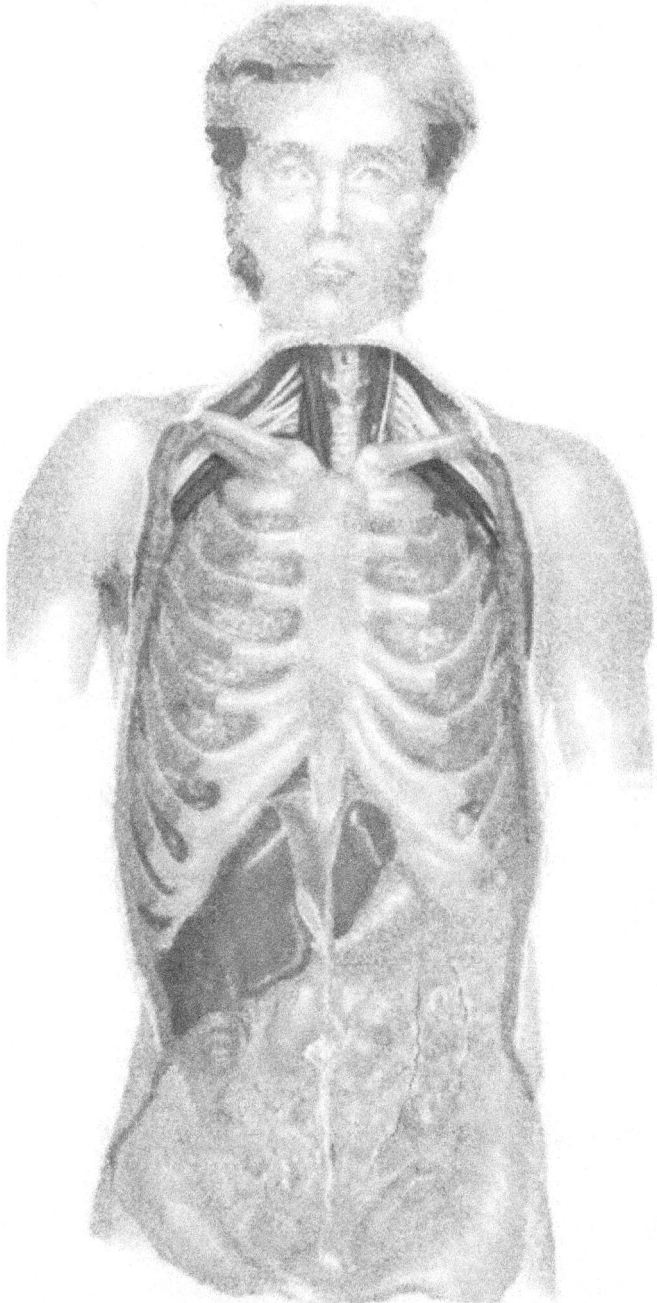

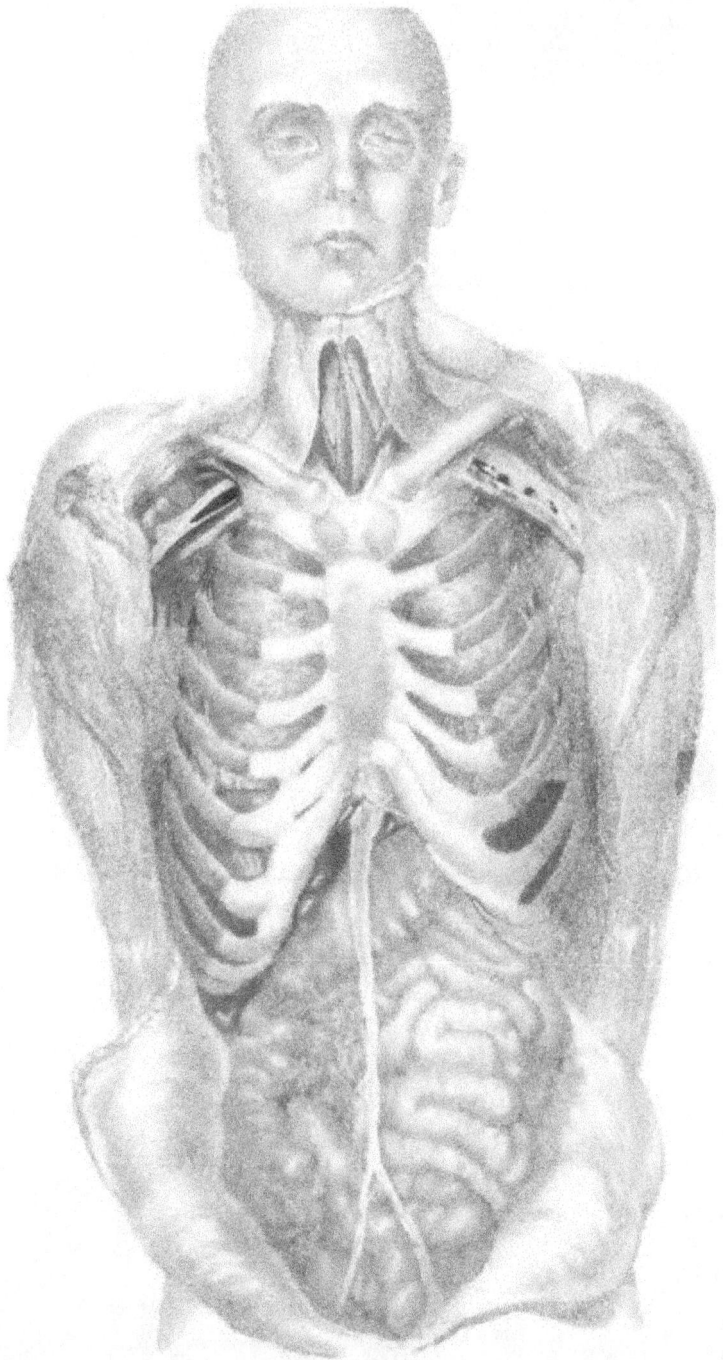

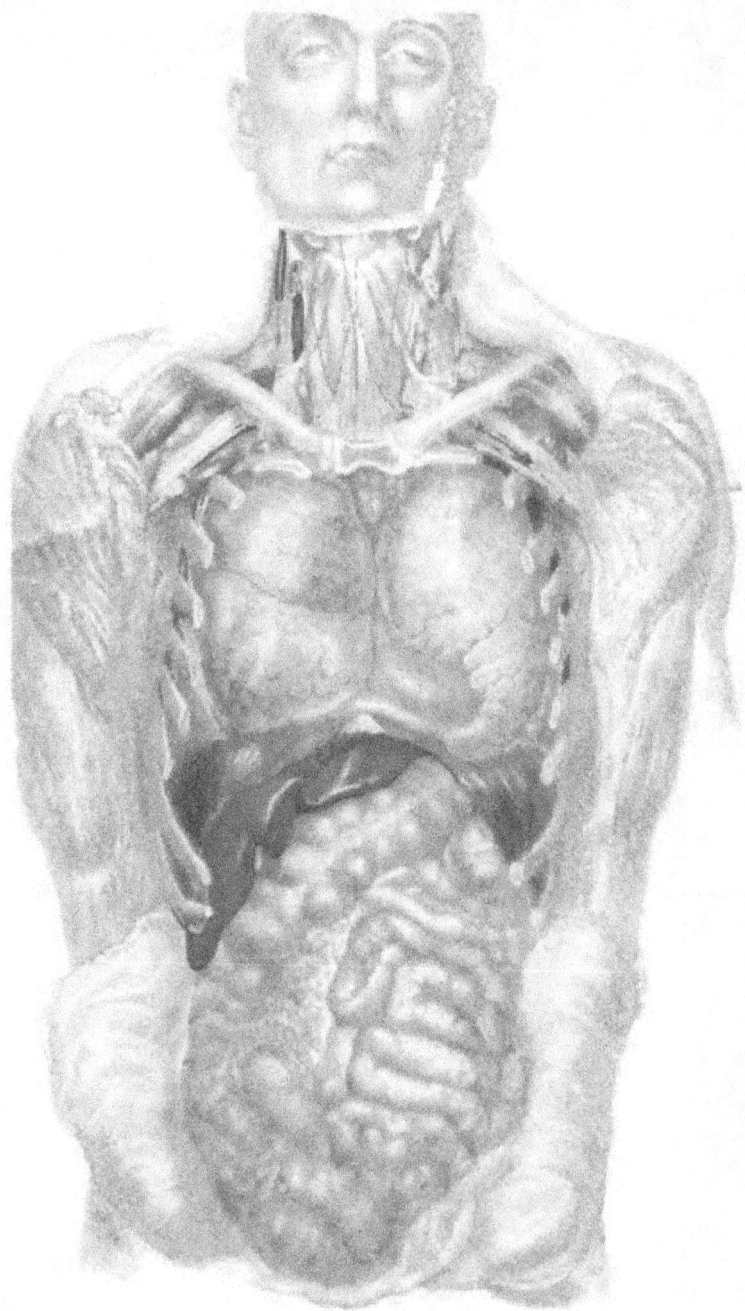

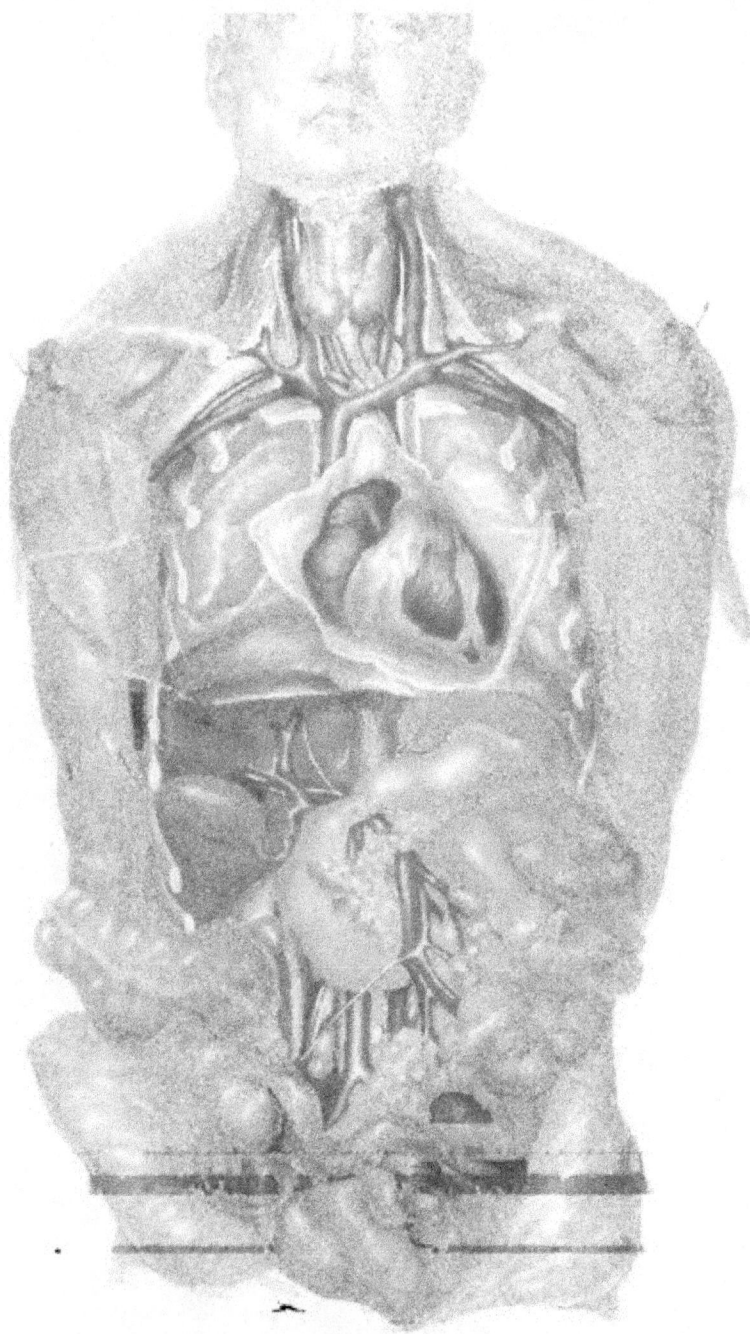

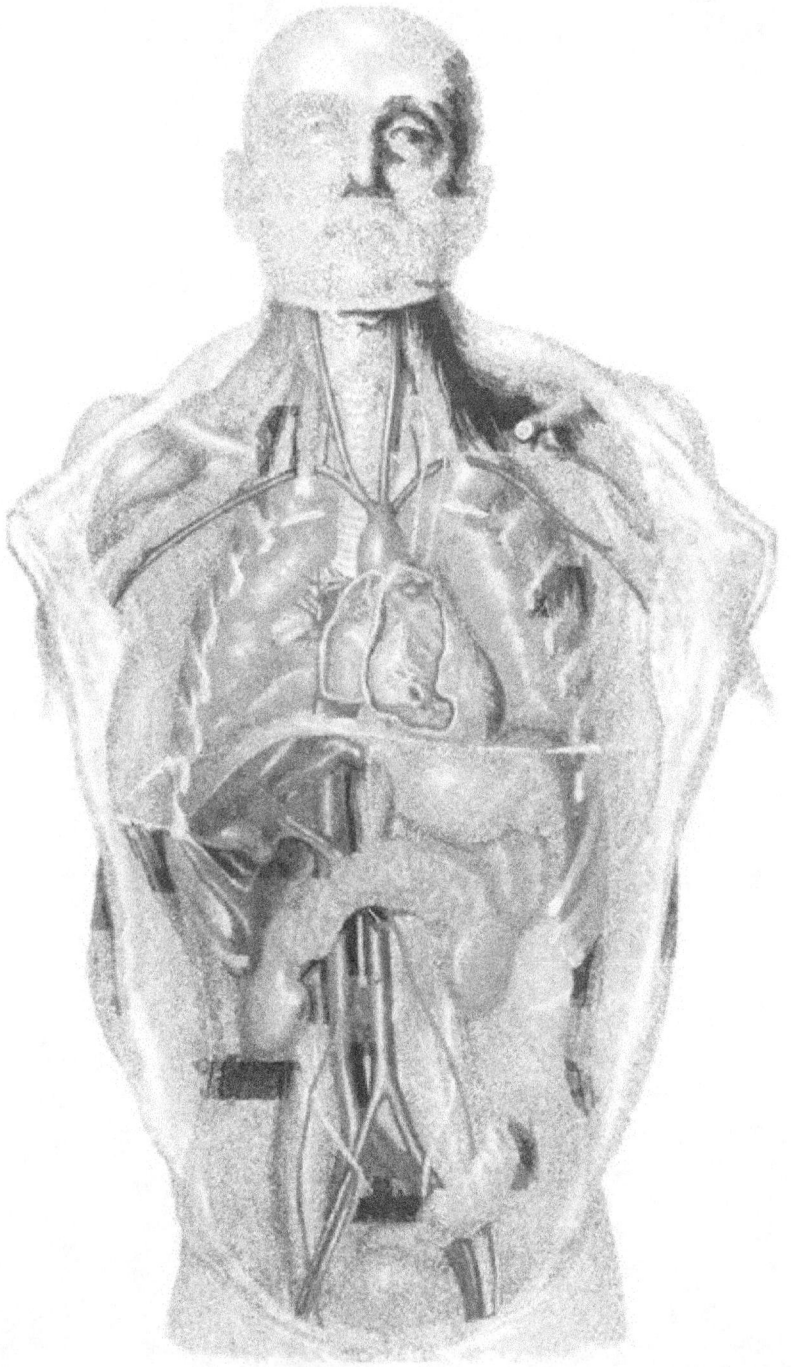

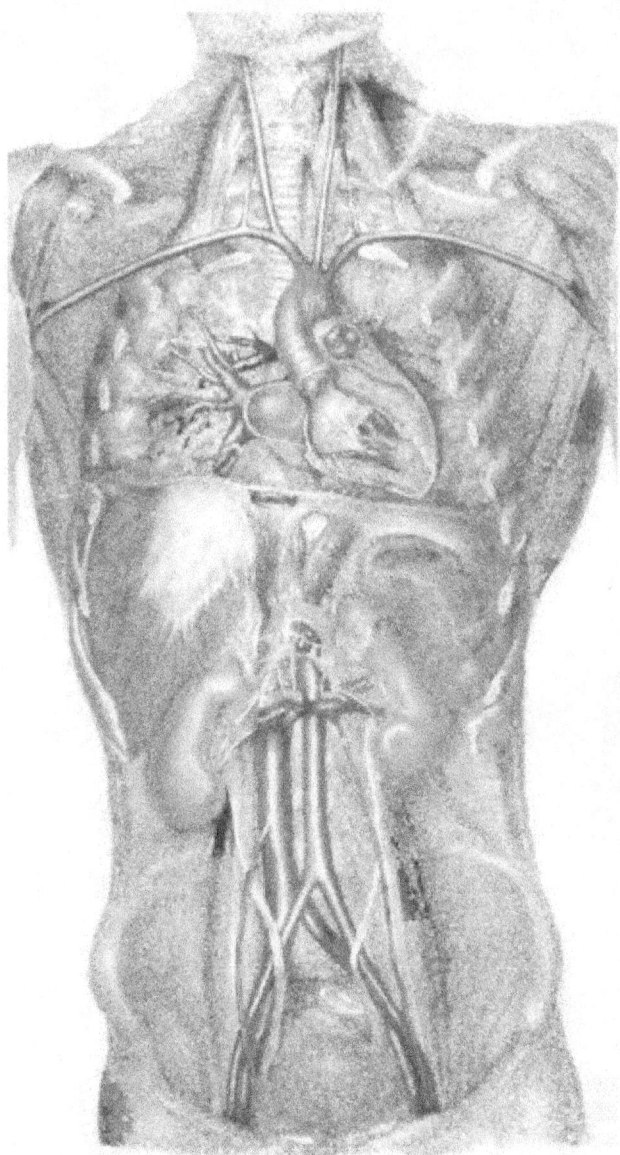

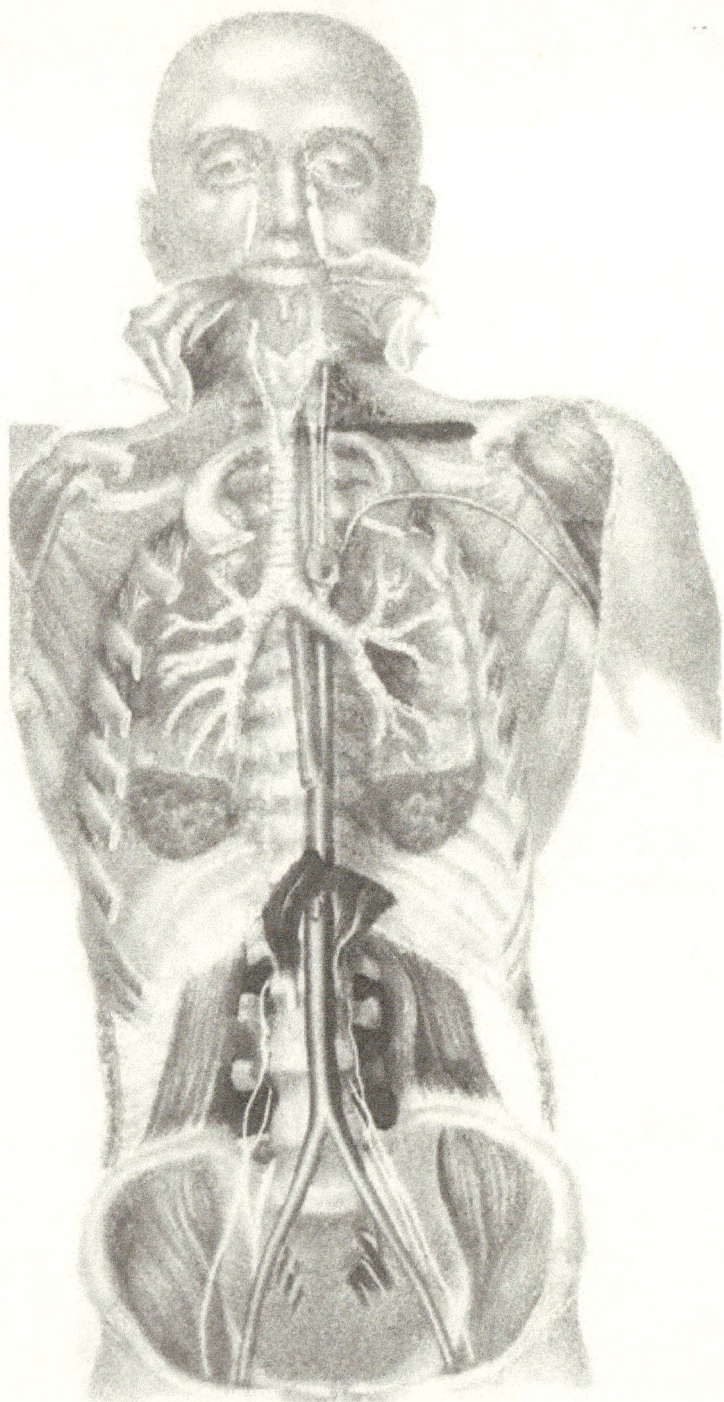

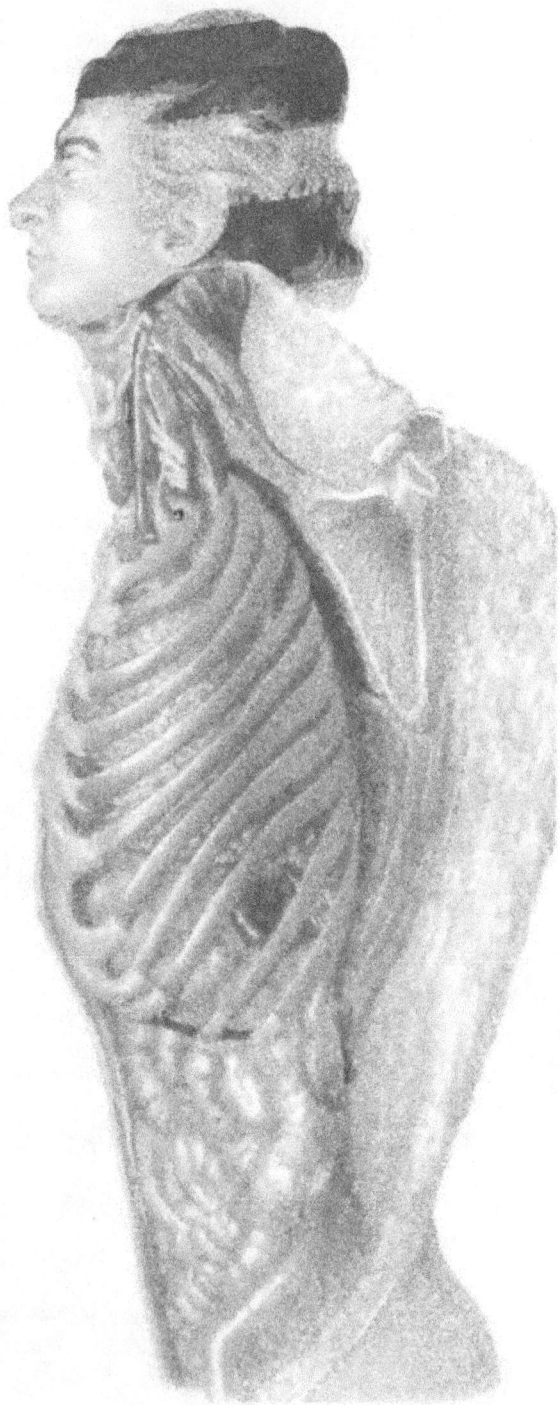

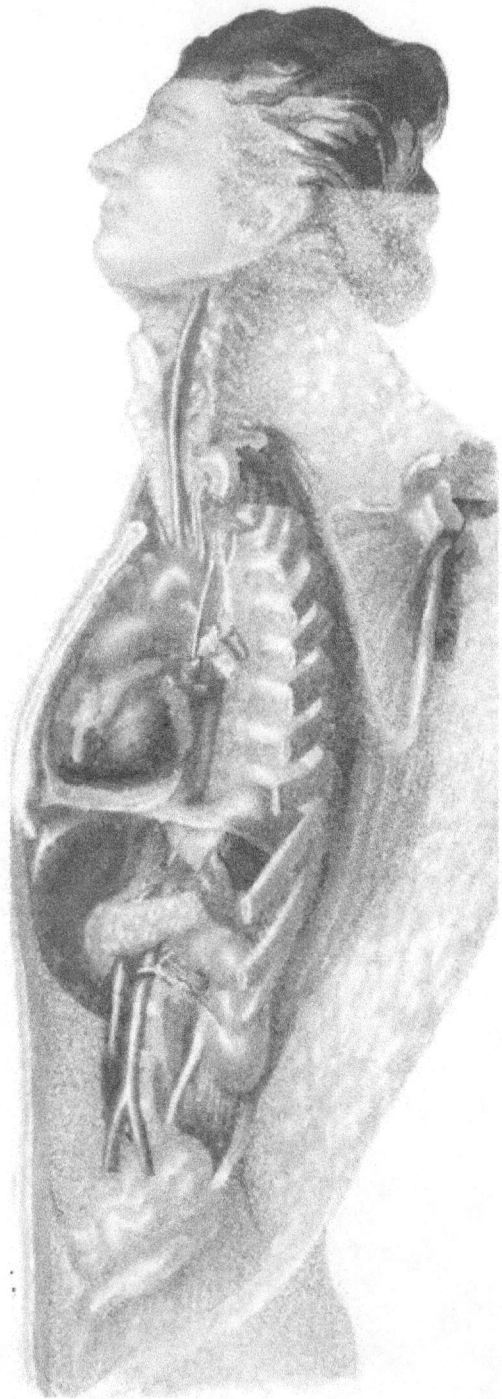

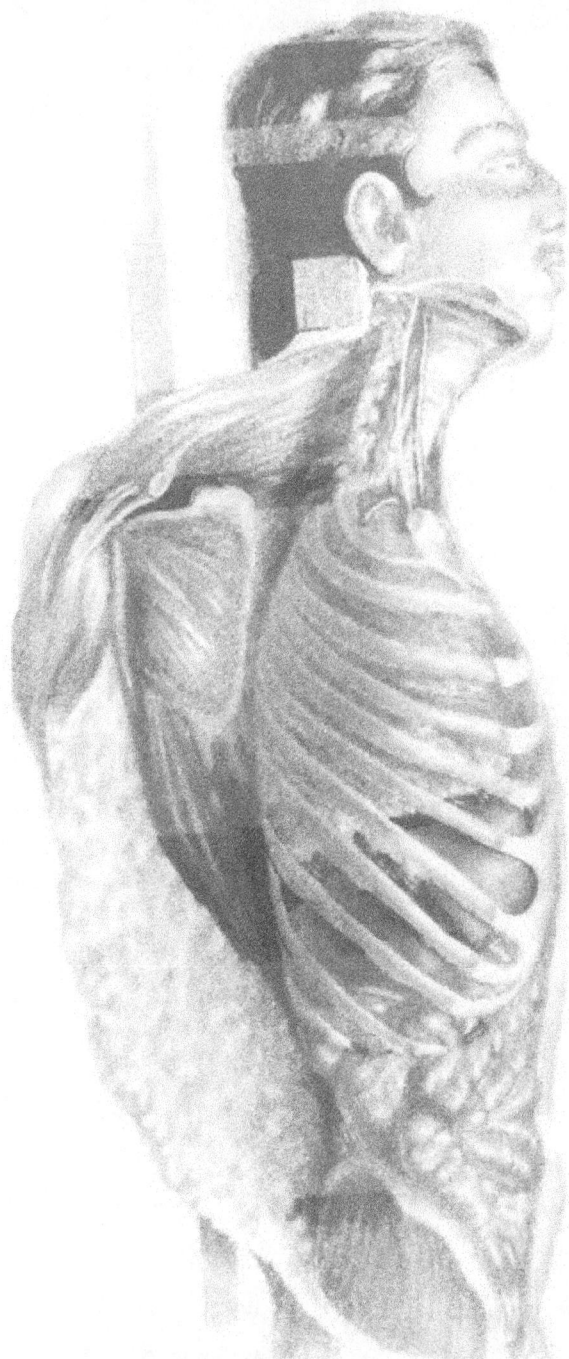

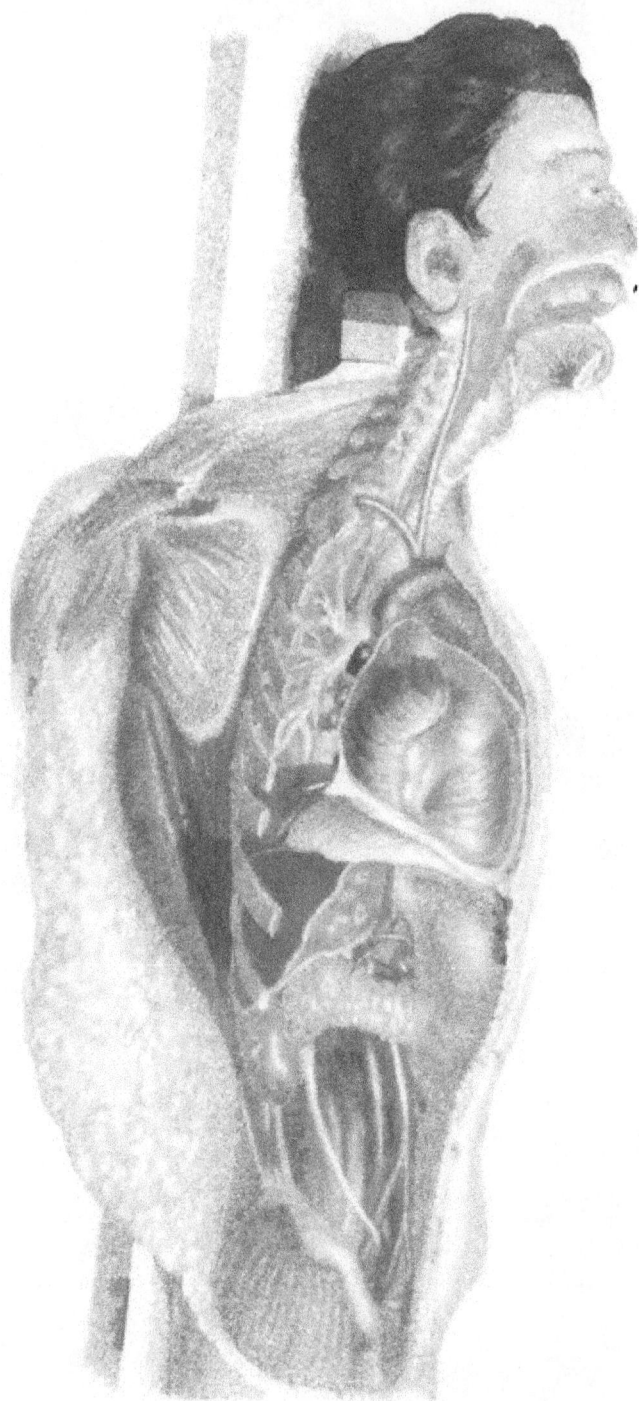

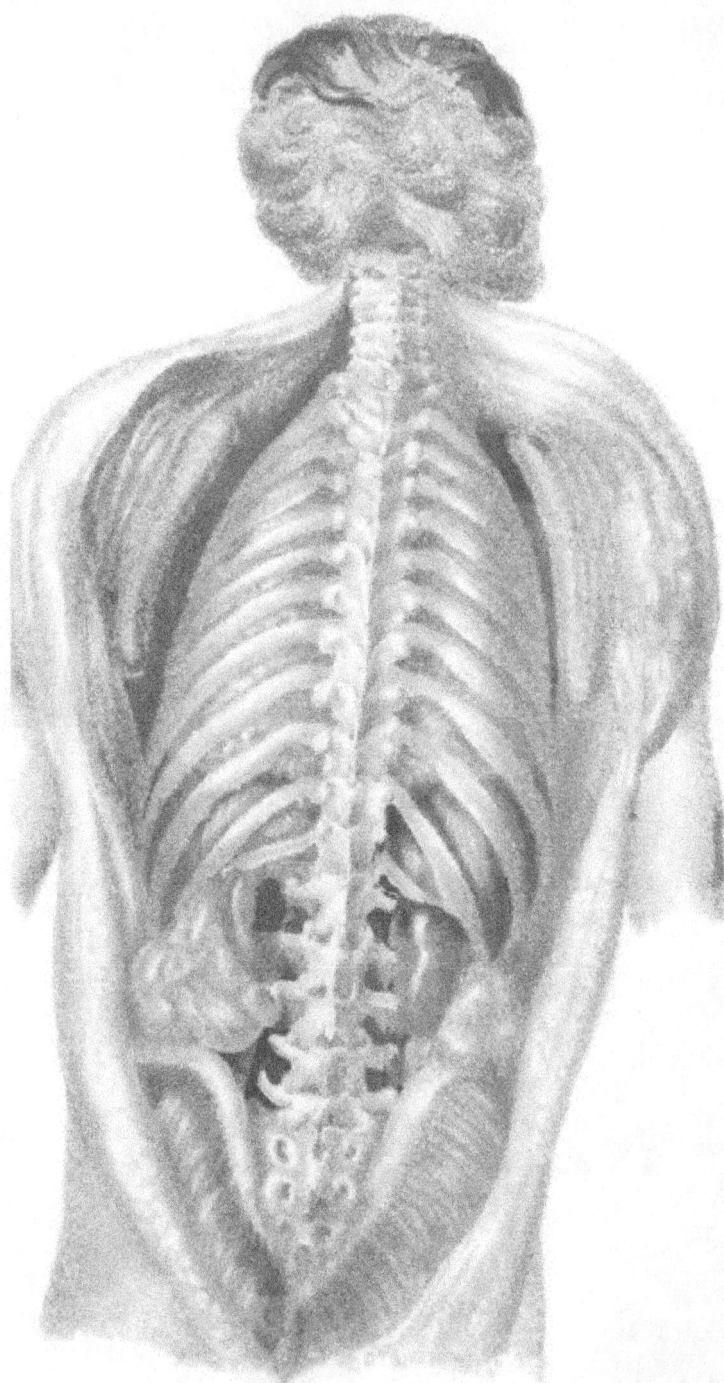

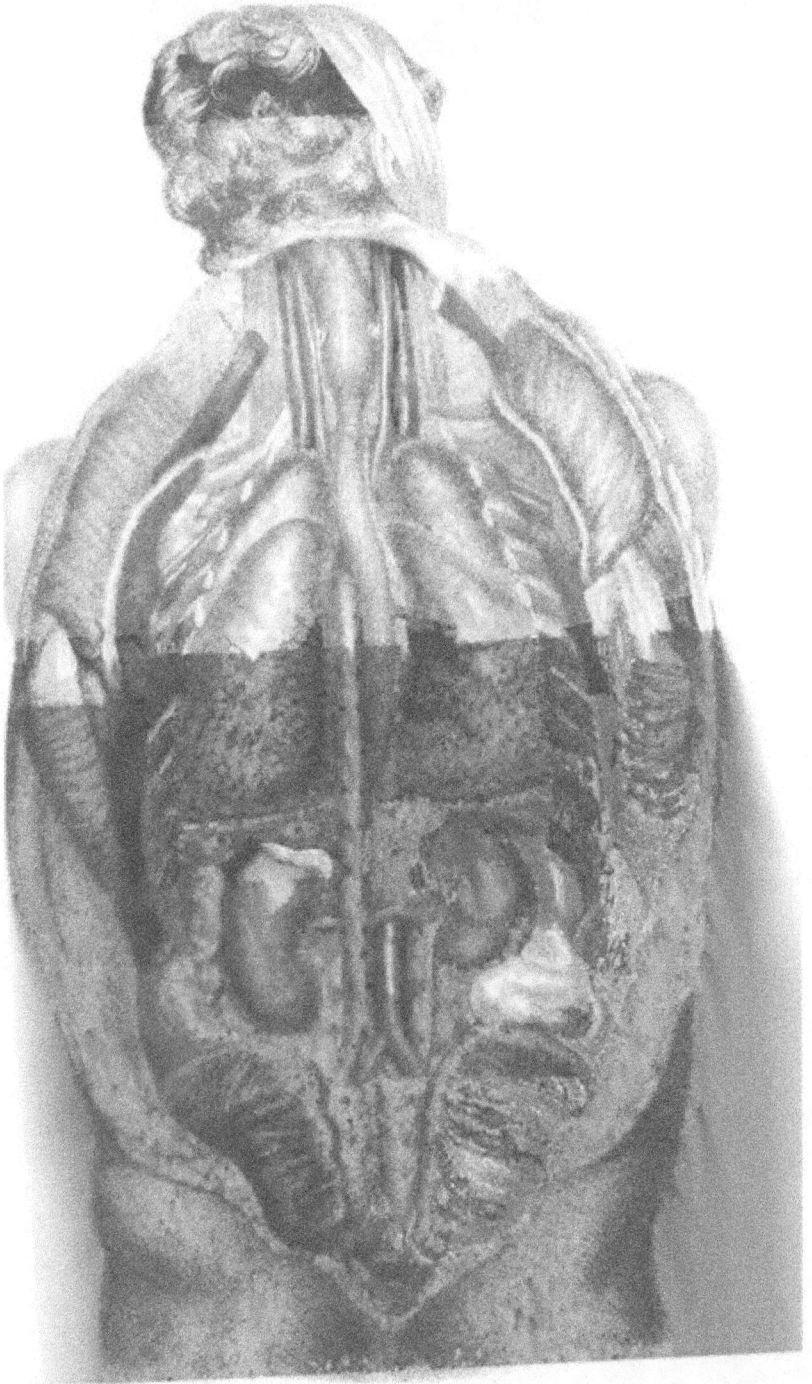

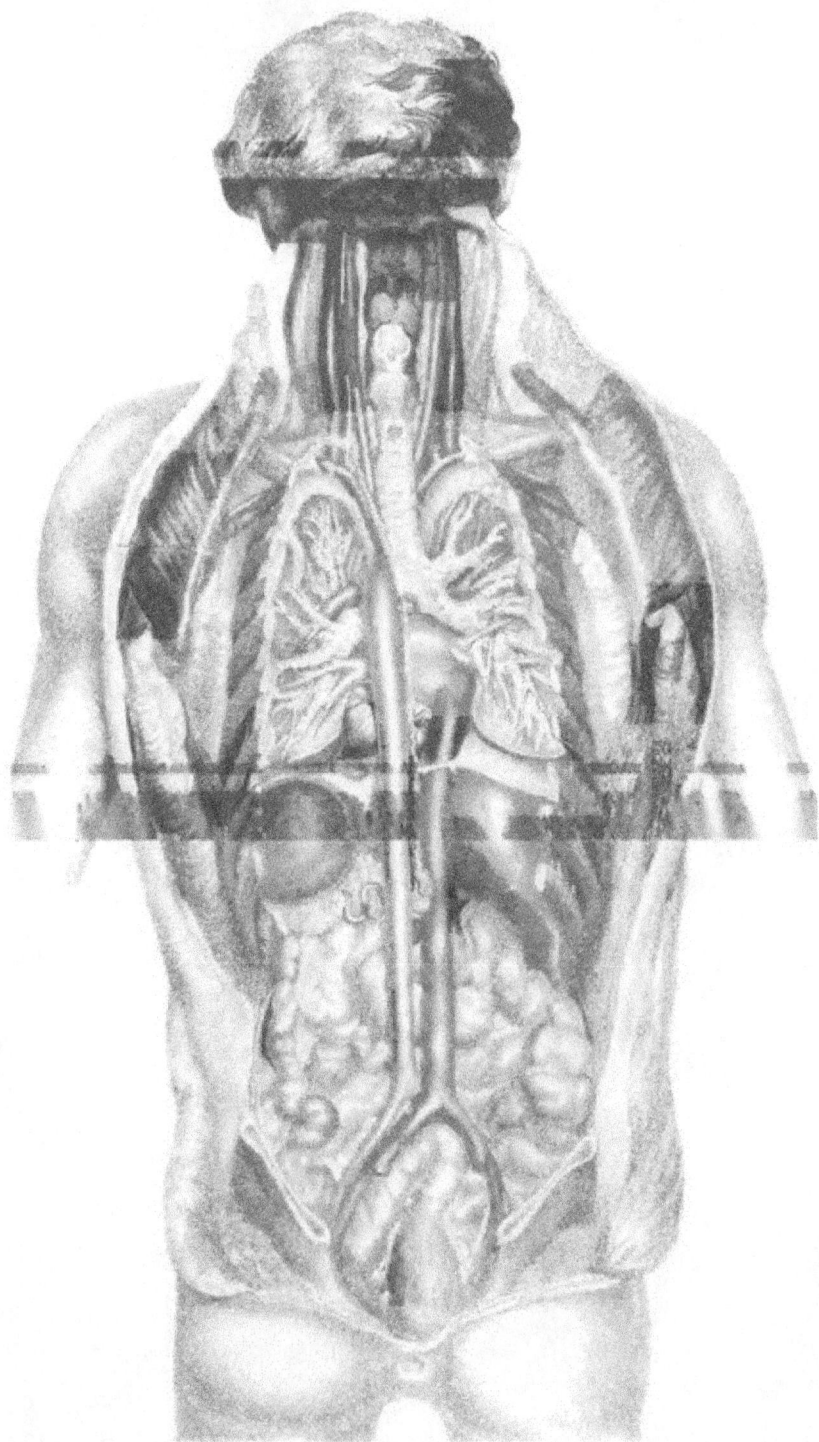

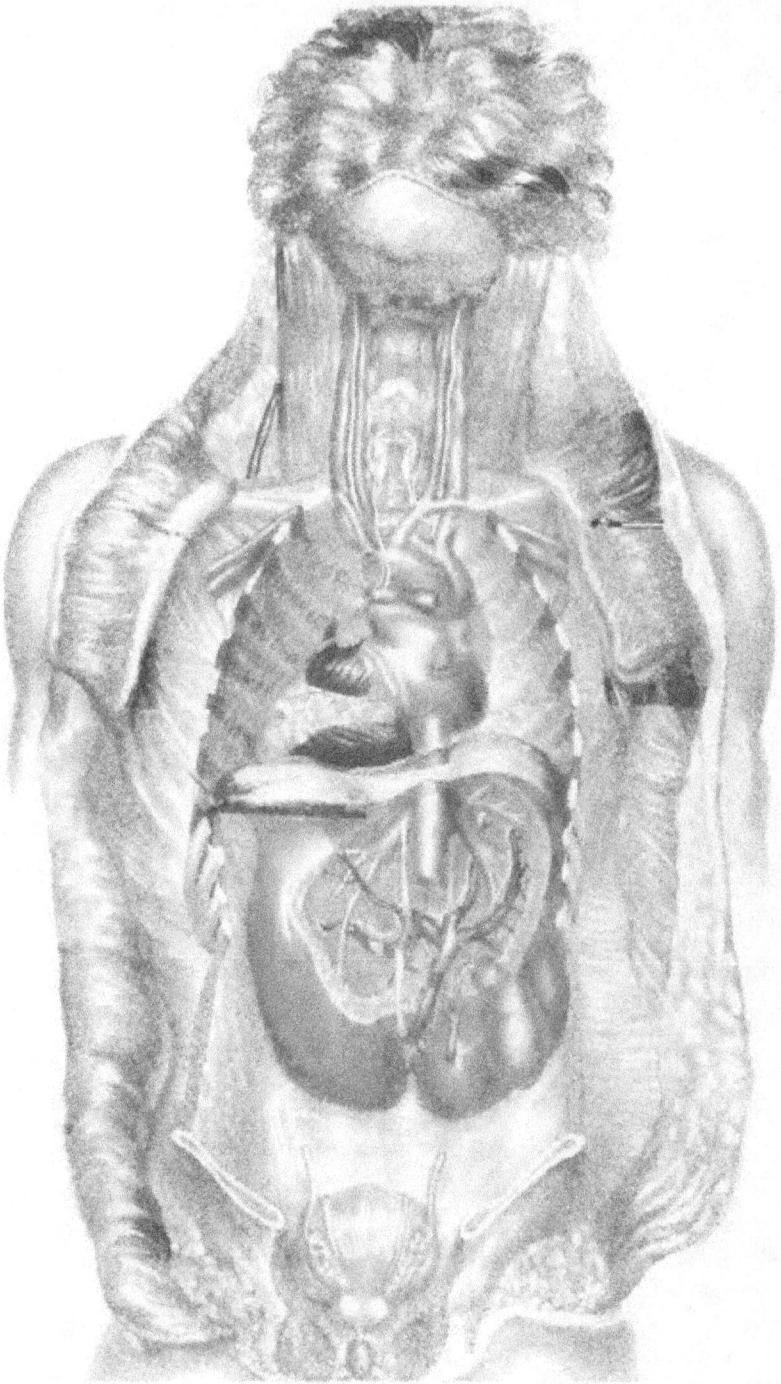

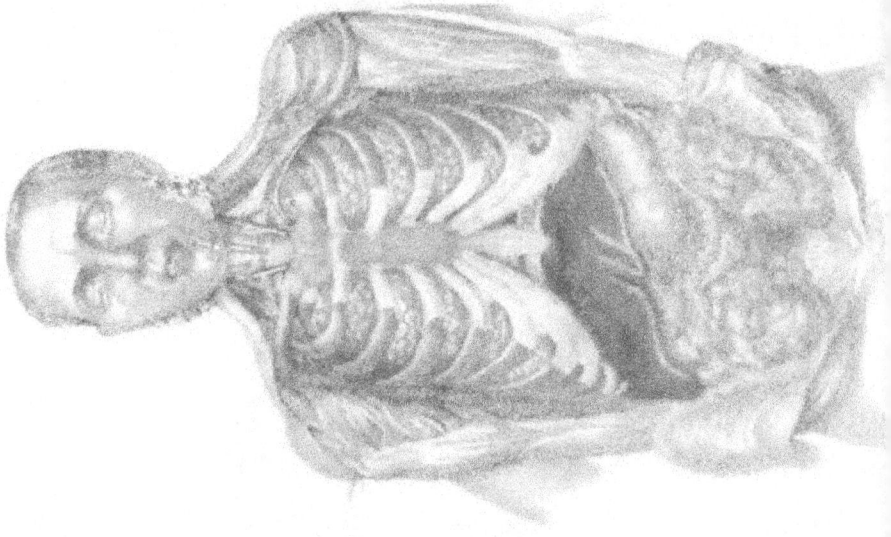

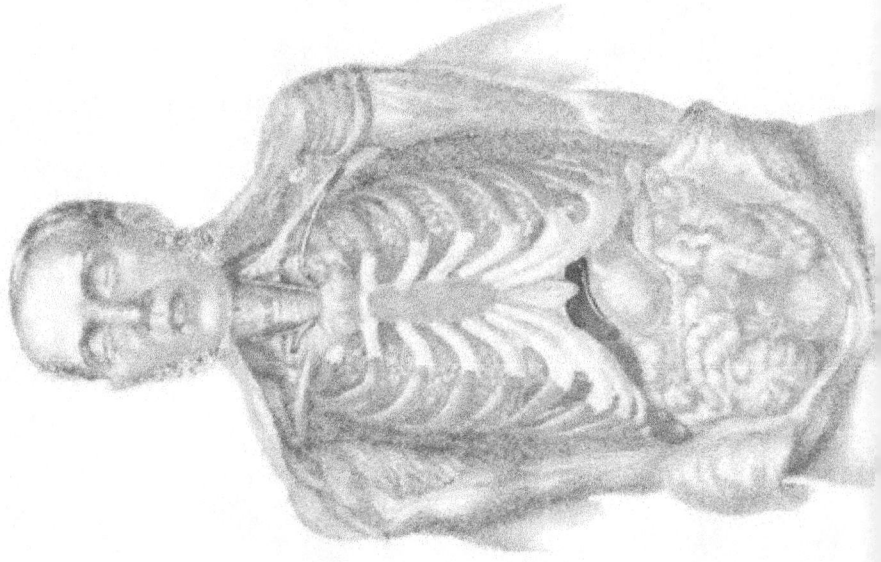

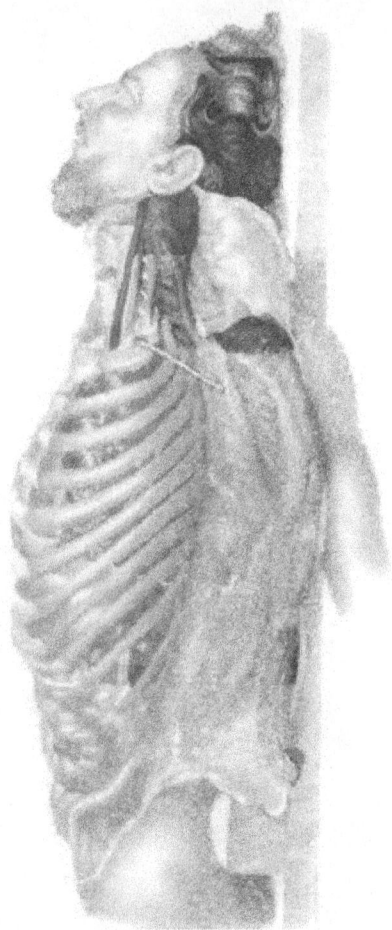

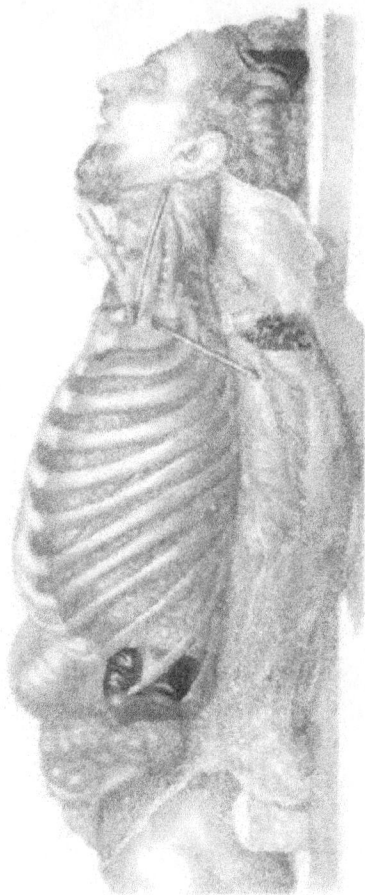

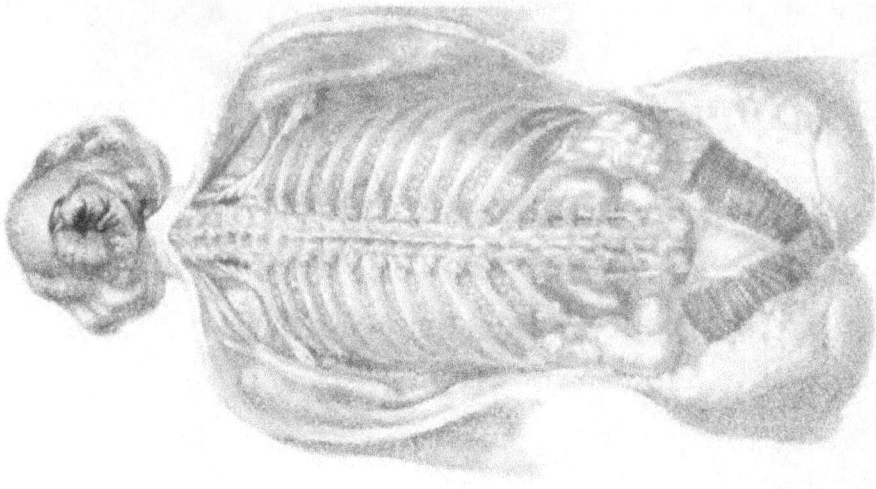

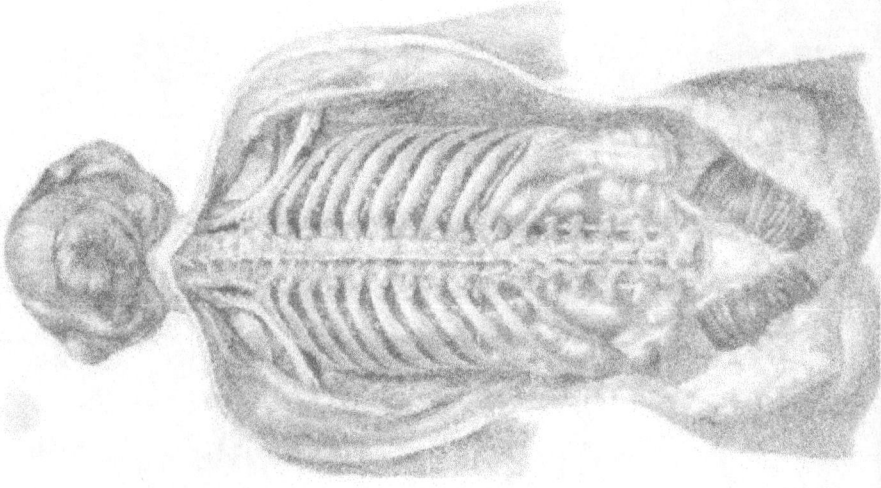

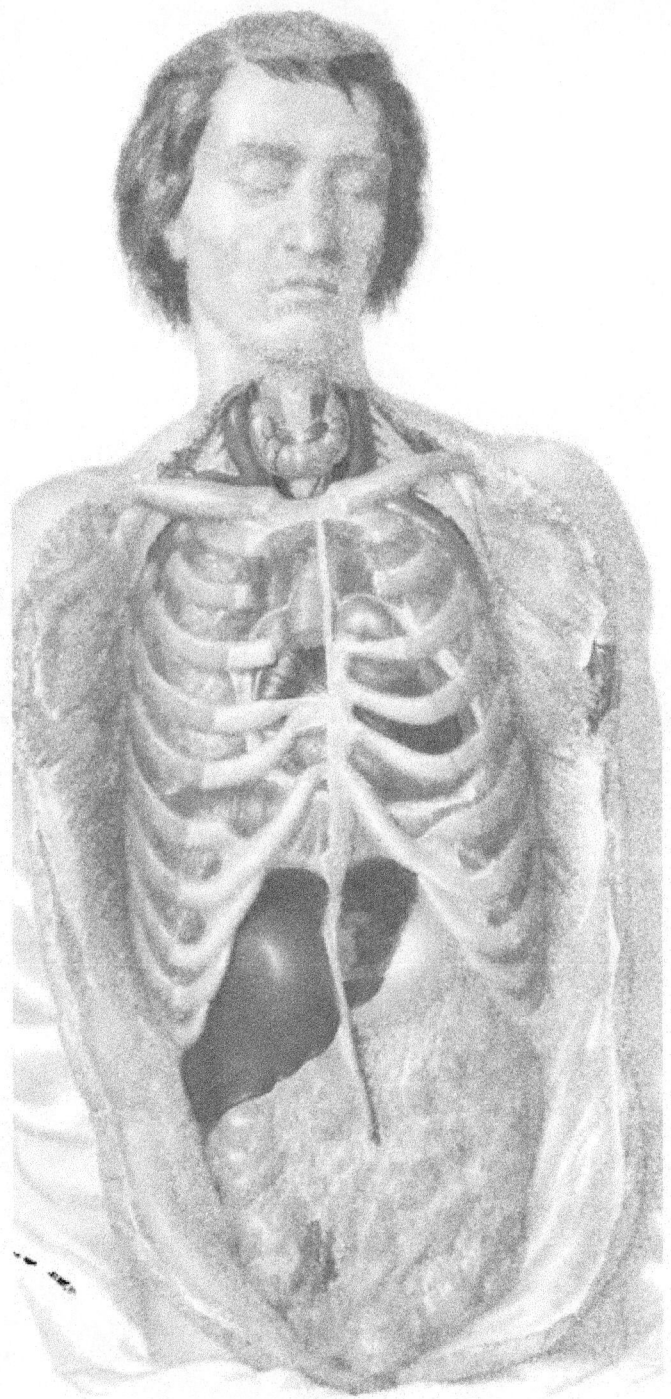

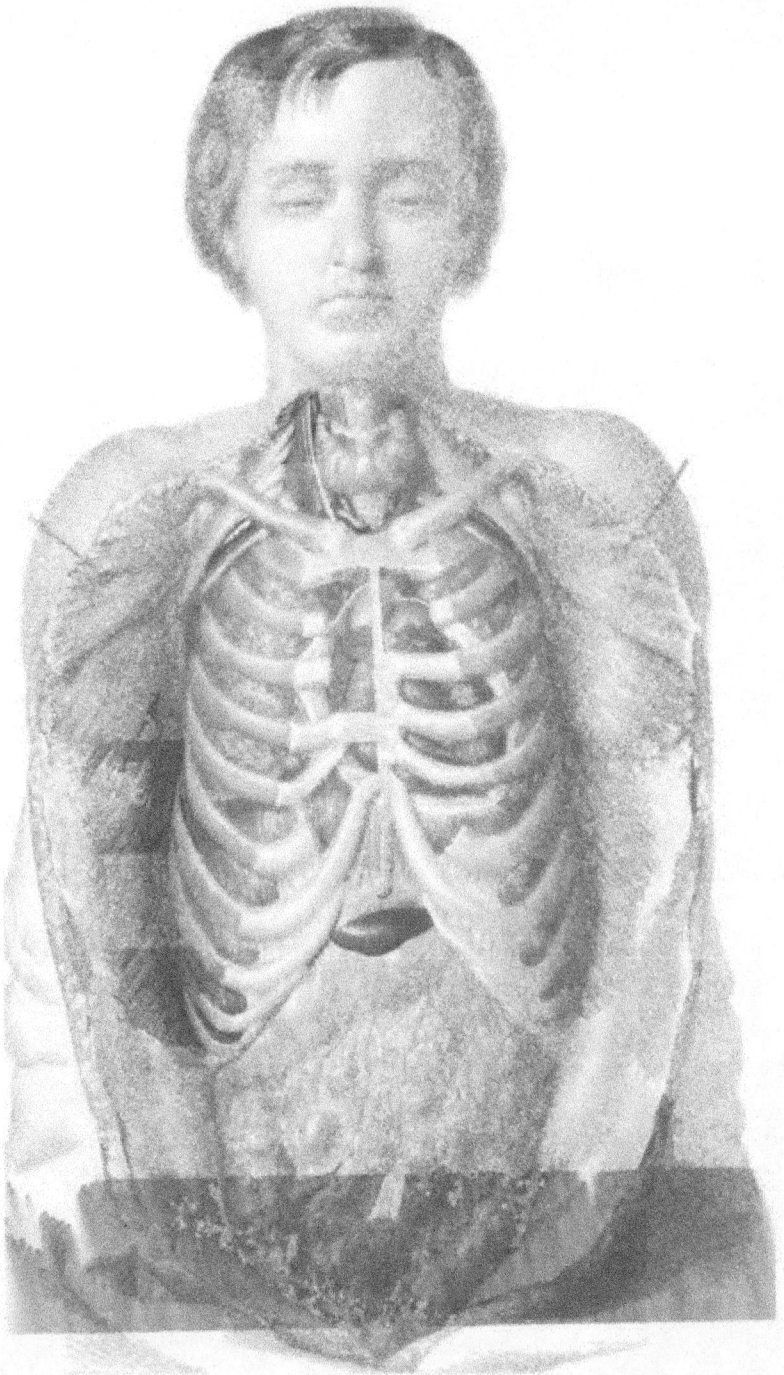

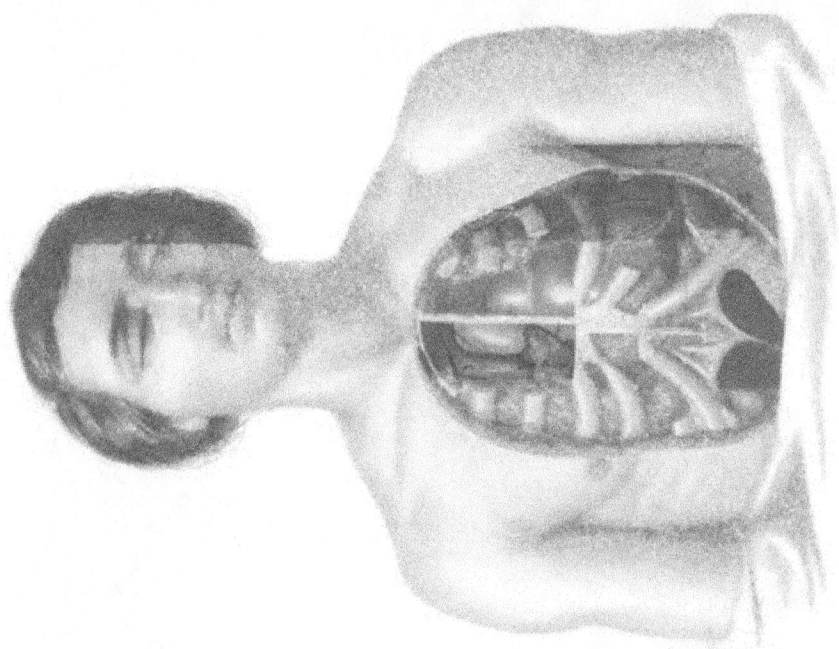

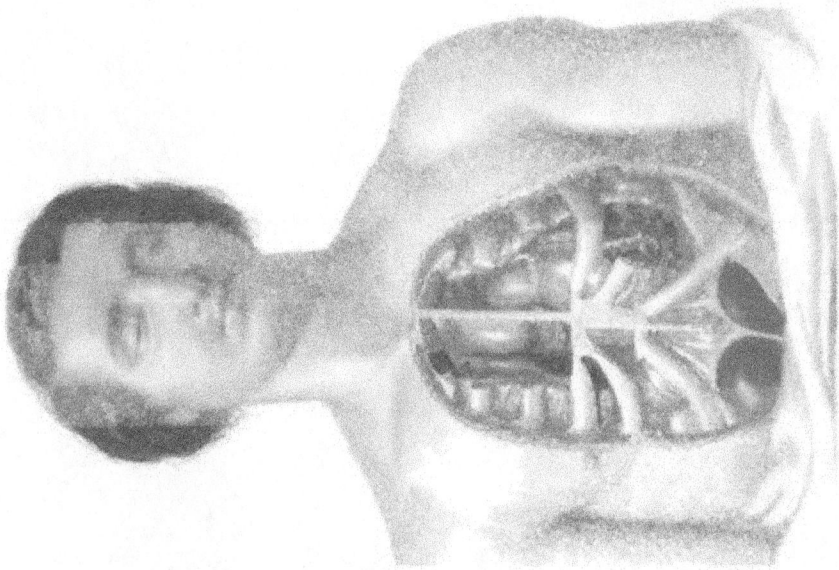

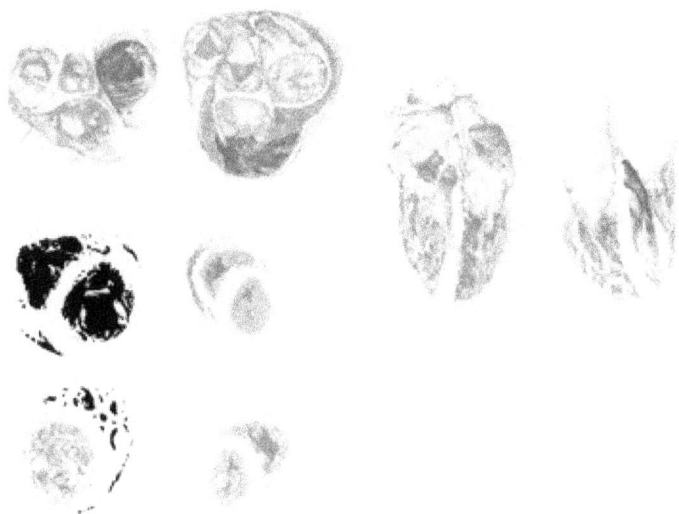

www.ingramcontent.com/pod-product-compliance
Lightning Source LLC
Chambersburg PA
CBHW031447270326
41930CB00007B/899